Out Of My Struggle
With Mental Illness & Homelessness: With
God Inspired Survival Skills

Out of My Struggle
With Mental Illness & Homelessness: With God Inspired Survival Skills

Nemasa Asetra

Nemasa's Book Collection
Published © 2017

Out of My Struggle With Mental Illness & Homelessness

First Printing:Year 2017

ISBN: 978-1-329-6236-5

Nemasa's Book Collection

304 East 7th Street; Austin, Texas 78701

Cell: 737-216-9078

nemasapeermhadvocate.wordpress.com

asetra45@gmail.com

http://nemasaasetrasbookcompany.webs.com/

Dedication

This book is in loving memory of my mommy dearest, Vera Johnson Hartman my adopted mother. She and my adopted father legally adopted me at birth. She was born February 25, 1928 and died of two strokes on June 25, 1995 is her buriel date. My daddy: Matthew Hartman lives in Franklin, Louisiana with my children near by in the same vinicity of St. Mary Parish region of the State of Louisiana. They are a variety of ages, sizes and hues. Some look what is referred to as a mulatto but their racial classifiation is African-American. They look very white or light skinned with either pronounced African American hair and Africoid physical attributes and some have very straight hair; lastly a few are darkskinned with various attributes nonetheless they are here. They are mine and I love them very much. I did not raise them due to extenuating circumstances but hope to have them in my life some day. I have only seen them twice, first event was at my aunt's funeral the second event was daddy's birthday party on June 7, 2014. I am a very proud parent.

Their ages are 15 years old to about 38 years old and I am looking forward to being with and near them one day. I contacted the Pro Bono Project to help me to secure visitation rights and to become a very responsible parent being that I forgot about them and suffered some memory loss and postpartum depression too. Pro Bono Project could not help me, their resources were limited and my concerns were not within their scope of practice. Also related to that spirit of the Lord let me know I did not need to go to that length to be with my babies. What I really need and needed was and is to let dad give them my contact number and address to contact me like they use to in 2014 on my old cell phone during the day. Or use my vital records information for a people search if they do not here from my adopted dad. Some things in my past are very vague and foggy it seems I have blocked out a lot of information.

Lastly, this book is dedicated to my lifelines Judge Calvin Johnson who was there for me as a means of advice and counsel with a very kind word or two while in the various hospitals that neglected and abused me, while in their care when I called him on several occasions. This book is also dedicated to Mr. Jim Letten retired U. S. Attorney for New Orleans, Louisiana. Also even though I know dignitaries and my cousin works for the department of Health & Hospitals, I still had to face my obstacles alone because some were ignoring me, meaning my Cousin Ivory Wilson and his colleagues I emailed for help and support as well as information and resources from the committees I had been apart of from year 2012 to 2014! As far as Judge Calvin Johnson is concerned he was retired and the other is an Assistant Dean of Tulane Law School who I either called or emailed for help to share with dignitaries who could become proactive on the issues I informed him of. Nonetheless I am not too badly damaged emotionally or mentally.

I am alive and well and I remain resilient, thank you Lord for delivering me from my chaotic crisis, amen.

To all readers you are appreciated for your support and for following me in my writings since year 2010. Thank you. Without your support and patience, I would have never achieved my dream of producing this book despite my limitations and my stroke on July 25, 2015 where Ochsner Health System failed to do their job and maimed me; they did not even address the stroke symptoms but instead dealt with the psychiatric care symptoms and tried to cover it all up in the process. Before being transferred to St. James Behavioral Hospital in Gonzalez, Louisiana I had a catherer put in while incoherent and also I was administerd some form of medicine in a small cup to keep me alive. I am not happy with the care that has violated the image of the Alton Ochsner legacy. Nor cast more shadows of doubt of the care patient's receive at one of the renown private pay hospitals in the Louisiana region of the USA! Just to think I use to be an employee of Ochsner Health System two and a half years and I am appalled that the staff talk to me in such a dehumanizing manner and scoffed at me because I was homeless and had no resources to take care of my basic needs.

"I am Nemasa and my story of resilience from abuse, neglect and homelessness are important because they initiate a path for proactive peer mental health advocacy in the entire state of Louisiana that can ignite activism that leads to effective change in the entire 50 Unites States of America and even worldwide!"~ Nemasa Asetra

Spiritual Inspiration to Lift My Soul

"Your word is a lamp to my feet and a light to my soul."
~ Psalm 119:105
A heart felt prayer from my Bible book from Cousin April Nash!

Dear Lord,

If it weren't for your word, my attempts to find my way in life would look like a dizzy person trying to find his or her way, blind folded. I can think of no better description. Thankfully by your word, I can discover your wisdom for navigating through life, which is so often in opposition to my natural inclinations. I'm grateful that you light my way today by what has been written! ~ Anonymous

May the Lord bless the hearing and reading of his word, amen! □
    "God Considers human reason, wisdom, morality, and even sunlight, for that matter to be dark and hazy compared to his word. God's Word is a flame that shines in the darkness ...if we use this light, then God will no longer remain hidden from us."~ Martin Luther (From Faith Alone A Daily Devotional!)

Acknowledgements

I would like to thank my Professors Dr. Paul C. Price, and Dr. Kwaku Person-Lynn, my African-American Studies Professors who encouraged me to do my very best and produce the best work I can in whatever I endeavor to do in life. I also wish to acknowledge my family without whose help this book would never have been completed with encouragement and support as well as understanding and patience especially my babies I have spent very little time with since their conception and birth.

The Lord is mighty and awesome. He never fails nor forsakes me. He is a mighty wonder and was there for me in the midst of my storm this year of 2015, both Spring and Summer in the midst of my poor quality of mental health care and healthcare Service at 10 hospitals and quite a few other mental health facilities in the State of Louisiana. Allllllll the private sector facilities include: Hospitals in Lutcher, Louisiana; Baton Rouge, Louisiana, Gonzales, Louisiana; Morgan City, Louisiana and Lafayette, Louisiana!

Hospitals
Partial Hospitalization Programs
Social Security Administration in Baton Rouge, Louisiana
Group Homes
Specialty Psychiatric Hospitals
Shelters
Non-Profit Organizations
Adult Day Care Drop IN Centers and Career Centers
*****Staff Members who violate and maim the mentally ill
Psychiatrist
Including Medical Director of Orleans Parish, St. Bernard Parish   and Plaquemines Parish including Chalmette, Louisiana!!!!!!!!!!!!
The White Male Dr. of St. Mary Parish Mental Health they call
Dr. Mac for Short/ Dr. Mclendon
Social Workers
Psychologist &
Psych Techs

Public Apology to Those I Offended

Dear Hearts,

Please take a moment to reflect with me on my events I experienced with regret but with a sigh of relief. The oppression that overtook me but did not crush me is the victory, because of it I am victorious in Christ Jesus.

What I mean is that God looked out for me and smiled on me as well as fills my heart with joy today. I want to apologize to all I lashed out at in the midst of a mental meltdown with foul, filthy vernacular as a result of my expressions of rage and challenges with humongous obstacles that were previously laid in my path for a little over 6 months. My reactions to these attacks via collaborations of demonic activities to destroy my mind mentally, emotionally and spiritually with battle scars that did not damage me permanently but linger with hurt, fury, rage yet a peace and the blood of Jesus rests over my soul and spirit as the grace and mercies of God protected me then and now. I publicly want to ask those deserving of an apology to forgive me for my poor choice of words and foul spirited unleashed rage that caused me to handle my oppression, abuse and neglect in an undiplomatic regard. It's my endeavor to continue to work on my shortcomings and conquer my angry temper flares with some much needed anger management coping skills and Mary Ellen Copeland's WRAP plan!□□

Preface

There are many reasons for this manuscript fruition! 1. People need to possess a boldness in life to share, discuss and tell their life changing stories to stamp out crimes, issues, and crisis that affect American society. Oftentimes people react to circumstances without truly becoming proactive as a result there becomes a breakdown in systems of society, especially the mental health system when abuse and negligence are permitted out of apathy, ignorance and selfishness. Thereby shoving the errors and corrupt under a rug or storing it on a shelf figuratively in hopes no one will notice until the next eruption and a repeat of the same investigation process report make light of the grievances and get off clean without any recourse or reprimand. With that being said, **I am telling my story as a self published author since 2010; to raise awareness that the Mental Health Systems in Louisiana are failing those who use them and primarily it's due to the unwillingness of providers to listen to the concerns of those experiencing it first hand. Another reason for this purposeful oversight is apathy and ignorance!!!!**

What I hope to gain from sharing my experiences in 2014 and 2015 is an audience of readers who will jump aboard with social, human rights and political advocacy and activism to alter and overhaul the infrastructure of the mental health systems within the entire state of Louisiana. That includes hospitals, clinics, non profits, jails prisons and agencies that contract with the state of Louisiana including day treatment programs. Lastly, and most of all that includes our housing like group homes and Independent living apartments ran for profit or non profit. Telling our stories is the only basis to justify and rally support for effective change. With that in mind I hope this work blesses your heart and mind to speak a word on our behalf. Of course I am no longer a Louisianian but my peers and their families or significant others are, so help please.
Thanks, Luv & Kisses!!! Muuuh awh!!!!□□

"Oh what we could be if we stopped carrying the remains of who we were." ~ Tyler Knott Gregson

To me this quote ponders what my mind can further become when I cease to dwell on hurts, disappointments and failures in life including rejection too. On August 29, 2016 I phoned my adopted dad and he sent word via his wife Dolores to inform me he wanted to part paths with me to stop calling his home the way I had checking on him etc. On yesterday evening I made peace in my heart and got approved from God to not get caught up in his foolishness I can not force myself on anyone nor can I beg someone to love me or accept me. So on this note I rise to the occasion to be a better person and love myself. I am getting free of my emotional baggage. I thank God almighty for freeing my mind and delivering me from the need to feel accepted by those that reject me because of my imperfection with a mental health diagnosis. □

Introduction

My Journey began in late 2014 around February when I encountered exploitation from some so called friends and extended family members. At least that is how they were regarded then. One of them, my former landlord Chalana Alexander- Landry and Ezra Landry who own the property that I rented under the Housing Authority of New Orleans section 8 program at 3505 Livingston Street behind the Plant Gallery nursery until I was asked to move so they could raise the rent under section 8, for a 2 bedroom house. I rented from them for three and half years and participated in the Housing Authority of New Orleans section 8 program successfully up until I got a new voucher for a two bedroom for myself and a caregiver for only $921 dollars. It was difficult finding a 2 bedroom in that ball park range in a safe secure non crime infested nor drug infested neighborhood.

I ended up moving and relocating to St. Mary Parish in Morgan City, Louisiana for a short lived move from August 1, 2014 to March 9, 2015. I had previously acquired my section 8 voucher through Metropolitan Human Services District who had came to some kind of formal agreement with HANO to secure vouchers for person's disabled with a mental illness. At the time I had all my documents and completed my application in the requested manner, as a result they qualified me for the section 8 program. It started out as a blessing later it became problematic because my Social Security Disability benefits increased from $1,100 gross to $1,500 gross currently which meant no food stamps or food bank assistance. This meant I barely broke even with rent at $425, utilities meaning lights only at almost $300 monthly and $200 for a caregiver salary as well as a little less than $100 for liability insurance on my Jeep Cherokee Laredo a year 2000 model and the upkeep and expenses of owning a vehicle. It was very difficult to make ends meet sometimes I resorted to doing focus groups or small gigs to help me out and it was worth it. However, it was a constant struggle.

The main point about all of this is that the Landry family placed a hardship on my ability to survive successfully and my life was never the same nor comfortable. However, it is a blessing and God is working mighty wonders on my behalf. I went from a power struggle with my former Organizational Payee: Pyramid Resources Wellness Institute and their employee Richard White who was rude and disrespectful and did not handle my financial affairs in a timely manner leaving me go an extra 4 or so days with a delay in getting my rent and allowance in the mail. He caused my storage to get auctioned on July 15, 2015 for non payment when he had the payment information from the beginning in an email. Directly from the storage company and with him listed on the storage billing account representing me. I had a brand new dryer in that storage that someone got for little to nothing it had me disgruntled at first but I got over it because my babies had all my important paperwork handed to them at my adopted dad's birthday party on June 7th year 2014 it was just material lost. As far as the clothes are concerned they got a few pieces from me and maybe the boxes of items I made and redecorated that were mailed from Ms. Lilliemae Cummings's home back in late June and early July. I feel pretty good about that decision to ship my items away and give my kids my birth certificate and social security card information and other important information.

Lastly, due to Richard White incompetence my benefits were thrown into suspension for 5 months. I was told by him it was due to a report that I had been in a state facility for more than 30 days. Social Security Administration indicated that it was reported that I no longer lived in the area he served on behalf of Pyramid Resources Wellness Institute, Inc. The dates without money was from 4/20/2015 to 9/3/2015 it was uncomfortable and inconvenient but I am an over comer. And I am victorious in Christ Jesus. Also I am ashamed of myself for getting mad at Judge Calvin Johnson and speaking words by text message and voicemail that were not respectful. They indicated both a lack of moral character and my crisis mentally. Sorry Judge Calvin Johnson forgive me for my words that were not very nice.

Things that transpired before I got myself together was 1. Homelessness literally on the streets from about June 20th or so after Father's Day upon getting kicked out of the Travail6:33 Inc. Transitional Shelter for resisting racial epithets and slurs from the owner who felt no disrespect for stating Blacks suffered nothing compared to her childhood and culture as related to the enslavement process and post emancipation discrimination action and inequality. I refused to cooperate with her ignorant belief system to dehumanize and discredit my people's efforts to fight oppression in America. Prior to that I was subjected to an attacker who showed his penis and sought to attack me in the mid of night with a knife. After my resistance and attack in the counter attack with my cane and fists he learned not to mess with me ever again with an attempted sexual assault. By obeying God and following his commands to secure my safety I was safe. I thank you Jesus and Lord God Almighty for safety and security. You are a mighty wonder. You continue to leave me in awe how you remain a deliver in my life in dangers, toils and snares, amen! 2. Got kicked out of the Baton Rouge General's Bluebonnet location for filing greivances around 4/15/2015. Then I got put up at a motel one night at a 2 Star * * rated motel by a psychologist who was in town for a conference in mental health that saw me sitting at a bench after hours. 3. On 4/20/2015 I was arrested for a lingering while forbidden charge at Ochsner Hospital for a diagnosis they said was scabies. At the time I was hoping to get in contact with my Cousin who lived in Baton Rouge to make suggestions how I could get picked up from Ochsner but his mom Hattiemae gave me the wrong number to call as a result, the East Baton Rouge Sheriff department arrested me. My charges were dropped on 5/13/2015 or so by Lieutenant Dennis Grimes. 4. Prior to that after leaving the Prosperity House Group Home on 4/14/2015 for not handling my business, stealing a $600 rent check for less than a week residence, opening my mail that was not addressed to him and justifying it in his own maleficence mindset then stating that my reporting to those who do not tolerate his abuse and negligence no one will listen to me because I am mentally ill. I reported his ignorance to the Attorney General of Louisiana via electronic reporting on their consumer dispute form I do not know if it was effective but nonetheless it was reported. 5. After this I went to the St.  Agnes Women's Shelter of the St. Vincent De Paul Archdiocese non profit organization. They attempted to justify kicking me out for not wanting a gay volunteer to get too friendly with me by touching me and bothering me when I was in distress. Finally my experience at the Bishop Ott Women's Center was not pleasant at all the staff were never in a character of compassion and empathy but rather patronizing, rude and dehumanizing instead.

With all that being said I am an over comer and have triumphed victory in the midst of my battles with a mental meltdown, crisis in the midst of homelessness, incarceration for a bizzare charge from Ochsner, and being without money because I had no Organizational Payee nor Representative Payee to handle my Social Security Disability benefits for 5 months. God is an awesome and mighty wonder, I thank you Lord God Almighty. Again I hope this manuscript that will become book number 8 blesses you like it is me with inner healing mentally, emotionally, and spiritually. Again please take note of the issues notated and become proactive with me to fight oppression, abuse and neglect within the entire state of Louisiana and all 50 United States as well. Thank you. Now brace yourselves for a memoir that will leave you charged to make a big difference in the lives of the mentally ill!□

As I move on to Chapter 1 ~ I would like to state and emphasize that my story of physical, mental, emotional and spiritual abuse and neglect at the hands of the various mental healthcare treatment team members, who act inappropriately in the State of Louisiana needed to be exposed so there will become proactive and effective administrative and clinical or facility infrastructure change. These are the persons who maim, injure, slack on their jobs and skill sets of both monitoring patient's and also remaining compliant with the established 22 Louisiana Patient Bill of Rights and Privacy Laws.

I hope that my sharing is a blessing so far and that you are in a position to speak up for effective change on our behalf. For change to transpire from business as usual to a powerful transformation in policies, rules and regulations someone must speak up so future caregivers, significant others will not have to stand for abuse and negligence of the mentally ill and the homeless.

Thank you for taking interest in my appeals to you the audience or reader to hear genuine less than perfect horror stories of crisis and eroision in the mental health systems; meaning: change, enough to foster effective beneficial results for all Louisianians!□ □

Anger Management A Work In Progress

Anger management is still a skill I long to achieve and add to both my mental health coping skill mindfulness character traits in my recovery journey and also to put in place with Mary Ellen Copeland's WRAP theory she is well known for as a peer advocate and author etc. By the way WRAP is an acronym that stands for Wellness Recovery Action Plan. Every person with a mental illness should have some form of crisis plan in place and work on its effectiveness with periodic revisions or updates to keep fine tuned with our ever changing evolving life cycle in mental health.

I recently developed my own affirmation and quote as a result of my peer sharing her own struggle with anger management skills. We both have commonalities and struggles with our tempers. I guess it is important to remember it is more important how we handle ourselves in the midst of anger and not act upon it than to beat ourselves up for the feeling of anger without acting on it which is better than behaving inappropriately.

My inspiration from Latricia my Peer at Lone Star Behavioral Healthcare Partial Hospitalization Program in Tomball, Texas

"Bad tempers will flare often in crisis but are only temporary; however it's more important to remember that it is not the anger that is the problem it's how you react and manifest in the midst of it, with that being said, I Nemasa can do all things through Christ who strengthens me, Philippians 4:13!, I will not allow anger to control me as a demonic vice or stronghold." ~ Nemasa Asetra

I strive to remain Mindful of the impairments my mental illness creates and overcome them with God first then the necessary recovery and clinical model coping skills like WRAP: Mary Ellen Copeland's Wellness Recovery Action Plan. It saved me and it can save you too! □~ Nemasa Asetra

This inspiration below ministers to me and I hope it will bless you too!

"But surely, God is my helper; the Lord is the upholder of my life." Psalm 54: 4

When things go wrong in my life, dear Lord, help me live out this declaration. May I entrust to you all that pertains to my life, even my life itself: from broken bones to broken promises - every form of fragmentation, frustration and pain that life in this fallen world can dish out. May I seek and know you as my helper, the upholder of my life.

Amen
Author of prayer unknown! May the Lord bless and anoint these words and may they not return unto him void and null! □

.

NAMI New Orleans & Racism At Its Finest

NAMI New Orleans is a non profit agency that prides it's self on advocacy, outreach serving and helping person's with mental illness it is known as a conglomerate monopoly over contracts with the State of Louisiana for services, treatment and resources in mental health. They are known nationwide but this particular region does not live up to their reputation of serving the people without an iota of discrimination, Racism or prejudice. My problems began with them when things got intensified in 2014 after leading a peer support group I facilitated on behalf of both the Mental Health Association of Greater Baton Rouge and the Bridges Program a peer led and inspired non profit entity of the Mental Health Association. While organizing and facilitating my Peer Support Group for Bridges the NAMI staff appeared to be very intimidated by the structure and format it was designed to empower us all and each one teach one mentality was the objective. I began to receive mean hard core stares of disdain and lack of approval while some of their words indicated the opposite of their non verbal communication. It was reflected in how they conducted business with me, for example, hovering over my 45 minute sessions with evil stares that mimicked unhealthy and unfriendly competition yet they have all the contracts in mental health because of the region's cutbacks in State budget funding not giving the total control and power to Metropolitan Human Services District any longer to facilitate programs we need that were ultimately done better but not cost effective. In essence it is and was cheaper to out source the work to non profit agencies at a fraction of the cost. My spiritual guide as an inner witness would not allow me to continue on the path I was on at NAMI New Orleans because it was not beneficial nor healthy for anyone. From my observations National Alliance on Mental Illness in New Orleans prefers powerless recipients of care who are not encouraged to maintain a high level of care. Meaning they need clients dumbed down without utilizing the concepts of the peer definition of the recovery model. Which is to reflect on our life experiences and draw upon our inner strengths to continue walking on a journey of progress of concepts that work best for us that demonstrate we comprehend our coping skills and are mindful of how to use those coping mechanism of the peer recovery processes.

It's idiotic to think that people will need their treatment less, their resources and services less, if shown self empowerment concepts, skills and techniques. Why would any fool want to dumb down the very people who so much need the help to maintain their recovery and a sense of wholehealth and wellness recovery concepts with an element of fostering resilience as the ultimate objective. My conclusions and observations leads me to believe it's to monopolize the programs contracts and to further fund their programs and pay their small salaries with their good benefit packages they brag on. I am not at all impressed with the NAMI New Orleans administration with such terrible fixated, one track minded thinking; that does not take into consideration what would occur if you teach prolific social skills and living skills coupled along with the concepts of the peer led and inspired recovery models and theories. Personally I think that if you showed a success ratio to the VIP' s and other like minded investors and contributors then dignitaries and others would be more impressed with their vision and mission statements to serve, and help in outreach, fundraising and educational resources along with some form of advocacy. That is real achievement. Anything less than this would be a joke. Unfortunately NAMI New Orleans in Louisiana is nothing short of a joke and a reflection of persons bent on passing on their judgments ingrained and passed onto them by their upbringing and social norms etc to the clients they serve and like minded coworkers and colleagues, it's so sad but it's a reality Racism, prejudice and discrimination are still alive and ill willed at NAMI New Orleans. I first became involved with them when I participated in their housing program at Canton House at 8316 Apple Street back in 2002 or 03. I lived there before Hurricane Katrina after the devastation I had to consider other housing programs because Canton House was not being gutted and renovated yet. I never did like how NAMI New Orleans operated and ran their programs they treat the clients like the derogatory term "special" and they actually think it's the norm in how they treat people, without respect, dignity and consideration.

Some of the staff needing a makeover in their attitudes is Angie, Lisa Romback, Grace, Deana Lainez, Ally Dever, Derrick and Cecile Tiebo.

As you review my public sharing please take a moment to consider how you may assist with revisions and implementation of their monopoly of State funded programs that are contracted to them.

Thank you for your proactive support in advance.

Beacon: Physical, Verbal & Sexual Abuse

On March 9, 2015, I was admitted to Beacon Behavioral Health Hospital for symptoms of my schizophrenia of my schizoaffective disorder and for placement into a group home. While I was there I was met with too much expressions of acceptance. For example, one of the female mental health technicians decided to give me a hug without permission and I did not react too well to it. On that same evening a male mental health technician called me baby and was looking over my body suggestively as well as always sexually harassing me, with viewing my body subjectively; meaning looking my body over: up and down. I told this Black male mental health technician with prison styled tatoos not to call me baby and to treat me as a patient; not as someone he was interested in sexually meaning desiring a woman. I was there for mental health treatment not to get laid. He never did comply with my request, instead he continued to do what he was doing and violated all policies rules regulations and ethics crossing boundary lines. As a result, my reactions were very furious filled with rage, meaning anger and my choice of words to deal with the sexual harassment was filled with foul words of disapproval. While there I wrote to many entities to inform others of his ludicrous actions but nothing changed.

On March 15, 2015 I was in a group session and we were discussing the two words Capitol like the main city or town of government affairs and the capital letter in a word and some got confused I suggested that the activity therapist explain the difference since they got them mixed up before I knew it I was requested to leave I did not leave was then handled by 4 technicians after 1 struck his hand at me and I struck back. Their actions next was to take me down by 4 mental health technicians and twist my arms and hands backwards as well as press my mouth to the floor and smear it. Afterwards It swelled and I developed a small inner fever with infection. It was reported to Mental Health Advocacy and Louisiana Office of Behavioral Health but my grievances were ignored and overlooked. On that same evening I contacted my mentor Retired Judge Calvin Johnson and he was very patient with me. He directed me to call Louisiana Office of Behavioral Health because his hands were tied. I want to take a moment to thank Judge Calvin Johnson for being there for me with a listening ear and for doing what he could to help me. Luv u Judge Johnson u are an awesome man of God I appreciate u very much. The final significant occurrence was the assessment comment that stated I was delusional that I was an author and that my books were on Amazon; my books have been on Amazon since 2010, as a self published author. Another assessment comment that was ludicrous is that I was delusional that President Obama was not the first Black President well if you consider the teachings of Black Studies Pioneer JA Rogers and his book The Five Negro Presidents it is very true. Finally had the ignorant Social Worker and Therapist checked facts and done their research, they would have seen that I have been a self published author since 2010. Go figure, I wonder where the mental health treatment team got their training from! Obviously they need to return to school, get trained again and go before the licensing board or committee. Honestly I do not think that Private Sector facilities are properly regulated. But nonetheless it's over with I got through it and I am not a damaged soul because of either the physical or sexual abuse or verbal harassment.

Again I ask that you would consider proactive efforts to knock out these types of abuses and negligence that were overlooked by those I spoke with via letter, Ann Boehner of Mental Health Advocacy that did nothing and the countless emails that were ignored out of ignorance by administrators including my cousin who was formerly the Program Manager of Office of Behavioral Health. It's beyond me to comprehend how all these abuses go overlooked and never challenged. Even though I no longer live in Louisiana it is still a concern of mine to get noted and dealt with for effective change to resort.

Grand Opening of The Algiers Mental Health Clinic

The event that led to my end in being somewhat of a spokesperson as a peer mental health advocate took place on June 23, 2014 at the Algiers Westbank Mental Health Clinic. The entire day was a disaster from a spiritual view point. I was temporarily staying with my friend's family and things were going on around me that were abnormal. 1. A car drove up with four senior citizens staring me down observing me then stopping and watching me as I got off the porch and on to the Regional Transit Authority paratransit ride. 2. The driver was dressed in a healthcare uniform which threw me off. I thought she was obscure for pulling up to the door dressed down in scrubs and not her Paratransit uniform representing Regional Transit Authority of New Orleans. 3.. The address on the new Westbank Mental Health Clinic was not the same as the invitation in fact the actual address was 3800 General De Gaulle however, the address that was listed on the email invitation was 3100 General De Gaulle funny thing is that they wrote over it with a piece of paper and taped it over the 3800 General De Gaulle I thought that was quite unusual. Lastly on this note there was no credit given to my participation at the event as a peer speaker yet I was used as a pawn to appeal to their dignitaries referring to Senator Heitmeier and State Representative Jeff Arnold. I felt like it was all distasteful in the one online article. They wanted to appeal to both dignitaries for funding, used my story of success and recovery yet they could not even state my name and my contribution. Actually that is how users do things since that time I have broken away from the movement let them find another person of exploitation I would not allow them to use me anymore. It's over !!! Now I see the bigger picture and sentiment of my peers who will not work for free nor give their time for special events in Louisiana as related to mental health. Now I see why some do not volunteer they desire to get paid for everything! That's a good policy for the mental health systems in Louisiana! I have not explored volunteerism in Houston, TX just yet but will soon. Another incident that was bizzare at the time was Peer

Support Specialist, Voncile Johnson asking me what my relationship with Judge Calvin Johnson, as if he were my man or something of that nature. People all he is to me: is my elder, mentor and role model the epitome of a dad or what I would describe as character and demeanor of a dad with integrity, honesty, stability and the image of a man with moral character.

I ended up not getting picked up on time by RTA Paratransit they came just before closing time and as a result all my disgruntled grievances got bottled up inside me for 8 weeks. After that I wrote an email and shared my feelings because that along with an incident at NAMI New Orleans called my mental status into question by peers who were not suppose to diagnose as certified peer support specialist like Nancy Roach Hughes the Conumer Liaison Specialist, Lora Bonnet and Carla Neely at Magellan Behavioral Health that was responsible for billing and a few others including a call from my former psychiatrist and a home visit by her and a representative in the healthcare field on behalf of elder Judge Calvin Johnson, a physician. This visit transpired on July 28, 2014 and that day too was obscure but it is not the focus of this discussion and chapter; I will discuss it in a later chapter.

The Lord is great and mighty, he never leaves nor forsakes us. He is a mighty strong tower. An armour of strength and power. He is worthy of all the glory, honor and praise!!! Amen may the hearing of God's word not return unto him void.

Inspiration from Lone Star Behavioral Health

"I survived because the fire inside of me burned brighter than the fire around me" ~ Anonymous

This is a very prolific quote for me because there are many demonic vices around me meant to crush me yet I am still standing against Goliath and that is powerful. In other words I am still victorious spiritually, mentally, emotionally and physically and my health has improved 100%. On that note many have come in my life to condemn me, judge me and ridicule both my actions and behavior as well as my deeds to bless others like sharing and giving of myself when I felt spiritually led to do so.

The fire inside of me represents my resilience. Which means my mindfulness or awareness of my weaknesses and my challenges then possessing the ability to apply my coping skills learned at Lone Star Behavioral Health PHP meaning my partial hospitalization program. Some sources of group therapy in Houston, Texas is derived from my Trauma Group, Emotion Regulation Therapy which is basically anger management skills, Process Group Therapy like for example Mr. Brad's ingenious idea of Narrative therapy a form of story telling, Coping Skills, Psych - Ed, Expressive Arts, Ropes, Horse Therapy on the ranch, Sand Tray or pretend play with an element of grounding which simply put is viewing our environment based upon our senses: smell, touch, see and hear; and taste. Finally, goals group is important to plan what I hope to work on weekly and then recap and reflect back on it on Fridays.

Jump Start Exercises to Build Resilience & my Recovery Journey, A fresh!

Exercise One

As taught to me in Psych- Ed by Ms. Kamara one of our Lone Star Behavioral Health Therapist!

Seven Things Mindful People Do Differently

*   Mindfulness means a sense of awareness of my signs and symptoms of my schizoaffective disorder and an understanding of the applicability of the recovery model and clinical model's coping skills!

1. Approach everyday things with curiosity and savor them.

2. Forgive their mistakes big or small.

3. Show gratitude for good moments and grace for bad ones.

4. Practice compassion and nurture connections.

5. Make peace with imperfection, inside and out.

6. Embrace vulnerability by trusting others and themselves.

7. Accept and appreciate that things come and go.

By: Elisha Goldstein psychologist and author ofThe Now Effect

Exercise Two

Narrative Group Therapy

It's a form of story telling in a process group where the group members put together a story; a sentence at a time with the participants using their creativity to form it, as well as, drawing upon their life experiences to shed insightful views of their inner turmoil with mental illness and their recovery journey.

Example:

Once upon a time, I was a little girl. I dreamed I was Cinderella because I liked the movie; then I bought a beautiful dress like Cinderella. It was to die for. I had shoes with diamonds and a pumpkin carriage. I was divorced from my husband. I went dancing to find prince charming wearing my fancy diamond shoes and my Cinderella dress. My two step sisters were bad ugly jealous witches that tried to keep me from finding my prince charming but I did not let it stop me .....

From the example you can see the ideas of a story forming that my peers and I brainstormed and formed out of spontaneous thoughts some of it is revised to make it more appropriate for publishing!!

Exercise Three

Trauma Therapy dealing with the topic of FEAR or Acronym for it:.
Forget Everything and Run!□

Questions posed in group therapy

1. What are you afraid of?

2. What is your biggest fear?

3. What about this is fearful for you?

4. What keeps you feeling afraid?

1.   I am afraid of disaster flooding and homelessness in the aftermath!

2.   My biggest fear, disaster flooding.

3.   What presents fear within me related to disaster flooding is my previous experience with Hurricane Katrina and what many experienced, homelessness , displacement and inconvenience along with uncomfortable situations!

4.   What keeps me feeling afraid is that disaster flooding and displacement is an annual seasonal occurrence in Southern Louisiana, parts of Texas where I live now and other states within the Gulf of Mexico region!

God creating me is the reason I coherent with a now residing in Texas after more  stability for am here and strong mind, Houston, than a year of ongoing struggles obstacles challenges and two instances of homelessness; because of my victories I am stronger and more resilient as my coping skills and survival strategies increase! You too can rise above in adversity! ~ Nemasa Asetra

Central City Mental Health Clinic & Dr. Katherine Smith

In 2014 I successfully got off Abilify because I could no longer afford the co payment with my Medicare "D" prescription drug plan instead I survived solely on my antidepressant, Citalapram a generic for Celexa and I was doing very well.   As is common practice of clinicians including psychiatrist like Dr. Katherine A. Smith. They believe that if you are diagnosed with psychosis then you absolutely must take a prescribed medication that serves as an antipsychotic for symptoms of voices, delusions and hallucinations with an element of paranoia. Well Dr. Katherine Smith went along with the plan to try just the antidepressant because it was not affordable but she urged me to contact her at the first signs of a melt down.

In my view, a meltdown never occurred but my stress levels were extremely high with the antagonism from the peer specialist I trained with for the certified peer credential in Louisiana and the jealousy and envy that built up from my growing book collection, the 2 committees I was on formerly in Orleans Parish, the speaking engagements and the networking and interaction with the legislatures including speaking before the New Orleans City Council and a few weeks later receiving commendations for it my efforts in sharing my story and experiences with my mental illness as well as the 100's of books I gave away between 2012 and 2014 to enlighten and educate others about the inners turmoil that tries to beat down the mental health consumer.   At the time I attended all my Continuing Education Courses in Trauma Informed Care, WRAP, Wholehealth and Resilience training, Ethics and so many more needed to remain informed current and impacted meaning mindful or aware of the issues affecting us the peers. During this time time I had to endure the unhealthy, unfriendly competition and strife that was building among the graduating class of Spring 2013 of person's in the field for the wrong reason with no clear direction just striving aimlessly. I as a result reached out to my elders about the issues for them to get corrected via email and where my long paper trail of grievances all laid out coherently became a topic of annoyance and an attack on my mental illness. It was very degrading for them to act so ugly and not read my concerns that spelled out the issues needing to be handled among peer to peer relationships by clinicians. What more does one need to know when all the grievances speak of the issues to perhaps meet on among clinicians and hash out so the problems don't mount. However they did just the opposite and let it all get out of control.   Dr. Katherine Smith ended up resigning this Spring 2016 and has not been heard from since. I gave her a terrible rating on physicians a website to grade your doctor and it was later removed. I still have a copy and will add it at the end. Lastly, I did a few Attorney General of Louisiana consumer disputes electronic forms later in 2015 and an ACLU about discrimination based upon disability but I was not taken seriously. I even added my grievances about clinicians and a peer, Voncile Johnson that alluded to Judge Calvin Johnson being more than an elder and father figure. It was inappropriate and I did not appreciate any of their accusations. In all honesty I am glad that the new Governor Mr. John Bel Edwards cut the Louisiana Department of Health & Hospitals budget by 70 million it does not benefit anyone when people running the mental healthcare and physical healthcare systems do not manage as appropriate we all loose. Some how Louisianians will survive some how. Forgive me for being in a mindset of approval of the budget cuts but what's broken is not working because those operating are only concerned with their own salaries, wages, benefits and retirement plans so sad but very true and prolific. Thank God for the new Governor Mr. John Bel Edwards I know he will continue to recover the deficit and do what's in the best interest of the residents of Louisiana that is both cost effective but also enforces stricter constraints policies rules and regulations!

Abuse At The Hands of East Baton Rouge Parish Prison

On April 20, 2015 I was arrested by an East Baton Rouge Parish Sheriff Deputy at Ochsner Baton Rouge, Louisiana for a lingering while forbidden charge because I did not possess the ability to get a ride away from there. I had made every attempt to call a relative that lives in the area but had the wrong cell phone number, called his mom Hattiemae and she gave me the wrong number. It was just a bad situation all around. Was taken to the central lock up and bashed with offensive language by a white male officer, who called me the "B" word meaning female dog without using inappropriate language in my publication. Next I was doing what I was told to do, going through my luggage piece from being homeless and carrying my belongings around with me. The officer shouted hurry up nobody is going to wait on your mutha f ' n a ** all day you get treated like everybody else. Not only that the officer was hostile and aggressive indicating that all though I had been in contact with Lieutenant Dennis Grimes and considered him as a mentor I would get the same treatment as everyone else.

At one time I was considering being a Volunteer in the EBR Parish Prison, as a Peer Support Specialist because I saw the need for it. I was at the 2014 NAMI Louisiana State conference and one of his sheriff's appealed to the audience for volunteers because the male and female population of person's with a mental illness was growing insurmountable. With an ongoing revolving door of repeat offenders and the staff was not equipped nor trained to deal with the issues of the mental ill consumers incarceration process in lieu of hospital stays because there are and were no beds available. The predicament arose when Louisiana Office of Behavioral Health would not approve it under my Bridges Peer Group and Peer Educator training and certification that they fund. I was very upset in 2014 because I knew there was a great need for them to be helped based upon my experience when I was incarcerated for defending myself against a man who struck me and led to my incarceration for an entire year because I was not fit to stand trial.

While at EBR Parish Prison from 4/20/2015 to about 5/13/2015 ladies got mazed including myself for requesting a shower in a voice she said was too loud. It almost caused me to smother I had to seek God and he led me to cough and spit out the saliva to get air in my lungs again. The nurse came but could not do anything for me at the time, so she said. There was a lot of abuse that was unjustified with the maizing of inmates that I never comprehended because they were not trying to attack the sheriff deputies. Not only that they were destructively Tasering the ladies that were loud or talking back do you see the sense in that. Before I left I did quite a few grievances and several letters and emails on the outside as well as a state of Louisiana Attorney General consumer dispute electronic form and an ACLU discrimination form for abuse of the mentally ill. Guess what, there was no response and nothing got done about the maizing and tasering atleast I was not informed of any reprimands, retraining or recourse to correct the matter. Honestly with the abuse of year 2000 it was different but not as intense there needs to be and overhaul of the parish Prison systems and there is a need for implementation of regulations to protect inmates who are not as violent as those who attempt to attack the staff!

I was released around 5/13/2015 by the Warden Lieutenant Dennis Grimes all charges were dropped and I was free to go. I did not have anyone to pick me up. They claimed they called my cousin at Louisiana Office of Behavioral Health and that there was no answer nor voicemail but I know that to be a lie because his phone always rang to voicemail in his office. The Warden, Lieutenant Dennis Grimes started to call from his personal cell phone but then paused and instructed me to leave the building and let the guard shack staff assist me. Now there are no free calls; you need a calling card to dial out. The female deputy used her personal cell phone and limited the calls on my behalf to two. She left an incomplete message. I ended up staying out there all day until I got sick with my blood pressure and an ambulance took me to Lane Memorial Hospital in Zachary, Louisiana. In the meantime I witnessed male inmates upon release being thrown out without their belts, underwear no shirt or shoes atleast 15 inmates came out with missing lossed items like EBR Parish Prison lossed my jeans and shirts never understood how a big old Prison system could loose people's clothing items they checked in, inside their storage area. Not only that being said, EBR Parish Prison had the audacity to issue me someone elses sweat pants with a hole between the legs and a sweat shirt. While issuing the items the African American female deputy was rude and disrespectful I was first thrown out in the middle of the night and later brought back in because I would not walk down the street like ordered to no man zone, meaning no where to go by foot. That deputy got called a dirty n***a as in the N word B***h B word for female dog for mishandling me. It was not appropriate and I want to take a moment to apologize to my elders for my poor choice of words in my heat of anger. Later that evening she and the white male deputy brought me back inside and held me in a cell at central lock up until the next day when I met with a social worker, the Warden and all the administrators who released me of all charges. It was an unforgettable experience I ended up calling Judge Calvin Johnson my cousin good colleague and friend to see if he could reach Ivory because the number I had was incorrect when two white women saw me outside near the guard shack and then offered to let me make a phone call for someone to pick me up while they attempted to lure me in their car. I told them I do not ride with strangers. And when I tried to make the second call to my cousin work number they said they had to go so instead an ambulance took me to Lane Memorial Hospital.

The period we go through in life in times of challenges, hardships and struggles is beyond me. All we have to depend upon is God alone. Now with all this being said, to reiterate please become proactive and share my story so that those forced into the incarceration process in East Baton Rouge Parish Prison can be free of abuse and neglect as well as fatal mahum injury and death at the hands of incompetent negligent sheriff deputies and other law enforcement staff! □

Thank you in advance for your input and your proactiveness to help those caught in the criminal justice system in Baton Rouge, Louisiana!

Divine Inspiration that Lifted My Soul!

Always Pray & Don't Give Up! Inspiration By Author, David Mc Casland

Luke 18: 1

Jesus instructed his disciples in a parable by analogy or a story the principle of prayer is important to never give up!

Are you going through one of those times when it seems every attempt to resolve a problem is met with a new difficulty. You thank the Lord at night that it's taken care of but awake to find that something else has gone wrong and the problem remains.

During an experience like that I was reading the gospel of Luke and was astounded by the opening words of Chapter 18: "Then always Pray and not give up" (v. 1).

Our Lord's encouragement to us is clear: Always pray and don't give up.

Lord in the difficulty I face today, guard my heart, guide my words, and show your grace. May I always turn to you in prayer.

Amen!

Remember Prayer Changes all things and makes them new again!

People leave you
out in the cold then
get mad when you
learn how to stay
warm by yourself
100 100 100

Old situations will pop back up
just to test you... Don't slip

Smile.
It intimidates
those who
wish to
destroy you.

I am at a place in my life where peace is my priority and negativity cannot exist.

Be careful who you call your friends...I would rather have 4 quarters than 100 pennies.

Look deeper at your problems and you will see gifts, lessons and opportunities to grow.

KUSHANDWIZDOM

Be careful who you trust,
the devil was once an angel.

~ Unknown ~

"When a man is denied the
right to live the life he believes
in, he has no choice but to
become an outlaw."

Nelson Mandela (1918 - 2013)

I have learned that success is to be measured not so much by the position that one has reached in life as by the obstacles which he has had to overcome while trying to succeed.

(Booker T. Washington)

izquotes.com

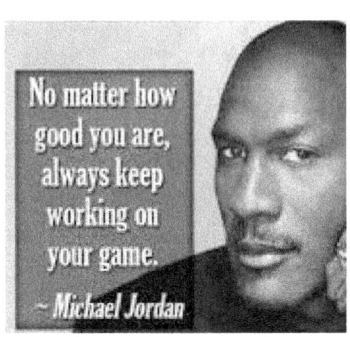

PUSH YOURSELF

BECAUSE NO ONE ELSE IS GOING TO DO IT FOR YOU.

KEEP YOUR HEAD UP. GOD GIVES HIS HARDEST BATTLES TO HIS STRONGEST SOLDIERS

FALL IN LOVE WITH TAKING CARE OF YOURSELF.

I REFUSE TO
ENTERTAIN
NEGATIVITY. LIFE
IS TOO BIG AND
TIME IS TOO SHORT
TO GET CAUGHT
UP IN EMPTY
DRAMA.

Never be good with not being
treated good. Don't accept what
you know is unacceptable. Know
your worth.

Trent Shelton

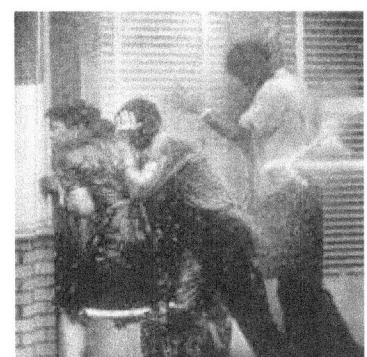

Thank you for sharing in my victory over a man created battle for survival.. Blessings to you…

We all struggle in life. And we overcome. If you do not know how to find your way. Ask God and he will guide and direct you..

Peace & Blessings, Be encouraged!! Never Give Up.. God is Great and Mighty And A conquerer over every e vil deed..

Hold your heads up.. Seek God and Seek Peace as I have and He will Give it to you..

Just a Teaser I will be back to tell you more.. I need this to start an official court proceedings from Louisiana to Texas and even into California digging all the way back to 1995 to 1997..

I am encouraged and I ask God to teach me to love the unloveable and forgive those it is hard to forgive.. Forgetting is not an option totally we must reflect sometimes that we not repeat the same mistakes in our life's journey's..

Ms. Nemasa Asetra aka Veda Latanya Hartman

304 East 7th Street

Austin, Texas 78701

Cell: 737-216-9078

nemasapeermhadvocate.wordpress.com

asetra45@gmail.com

Maslow's (1943, 1954) hierarchy of needs is a motivational theory in psychology comprising a five tier model of human needs, often depicted as hierarchical levels within a pyramid. ... Our most basic need is for physical survival, and this will be the first thing that motivates our behaviour.

Maslow's Hierarchy of Needs | Simply Psychology

www.simplypsychology.org/maslow.html

Maslow Theory of the 5 Basic Needs Not Wants

Seek God First and He shall Supply you all your needs and increase
you with wants just as the bible the blueprint for living speaks
of...Smile.. lol : laugh out loud.. God hears I have sought
him.. I cried out to him.. It was hard to hear him .. it's a
personal walk you will find him just as I did and still doooo...
Be encouraged.

Blessings... smile.....

Ms. Nemasa Asetra aka Veda Latanya Hartman

Little Ms. Mildred and Ms. Americanized Farrakahna

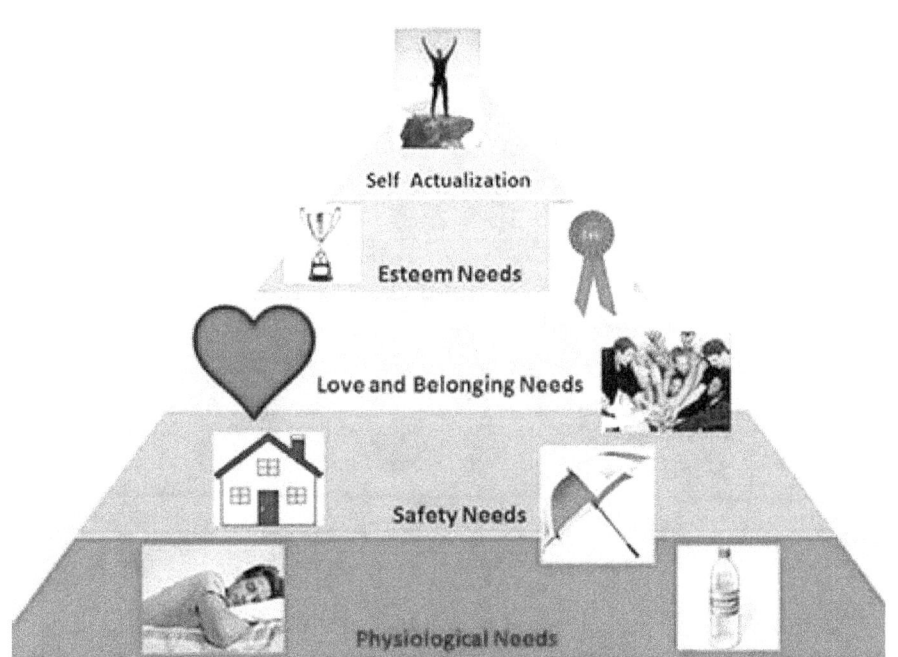

www.ingramcontent.com/pod-product-compliance
Lightning Source LLC
Chambersburg PA
CBHW081850280526
45789CB00007B/2637